IMAGES
of America

LA JOLLA

ON THE COVER. Beautiful ocean vistas attracted visitors to La Jolla from the beginning. In the early 20th century, they arrived by train to take in the sea breezes and search for shells and fossils along the beaches. These people ultimately remained to build houses and cottages along the cliffs above the endless blue Pacific.

IMAGES
of America

LA JOLLA

Carol Olten, Heather Kuhn,
and the La Jolla Historical Society

ARCADIA
PUBLISHING

Published by Arcadia Publishing
Charleston SC, Chicago IL, Portsmouth NH, San Francisco CA

Library of Congress Catalog Card Number: 2007939177

For all general information contact Arcadia Publishing at:
Telephone 843-853-2070
Fax 843-853-0044
E-mail sales@arcadiapublishing.com
For customer service and orders:
Toll-Free 1-888-313-2665

Visit us on the Internet at www.arcadiapublishing.com

This book is dedicated to the diverse group of pioneers who first sought La Jolla as their home and made it into an exceptional community devoted to education, culture, and the growth of the human spirit. Without their efforts, La Jolla's history would be far different than it is today.

CONTENTS

ACKNOWLEDGMENTS

The photographs used in this book come exclusively from the archives of the La Jolla Historical Society, a collection of more than 10,000 images dating from the 1880s to the present day. We would like to additionally acknowledge the hundreds of people—volunteers, staff, administrators, and board members—who have helped to assemble the collection and preserve it for posterity. The society was founded in 1963 by a small group of citizens who were concerned that La Jolla was losing its early historical roots. Their efforts led to the formation of a highly viable organization devoted not only to preservation, but to La Jolla's future as a continuing community. We would also like to thank the many supporters and patrons who have given generously in time and money to sustain our present and future programs.

Without the following La Jolla historical figures, we would have far less interesting material: Francis Terrell Botsford, the "Father of La Jolla," who purchased the first lots and laid out the plans for the initial village in 1887; Anna Held, the creative spirit who began the Green Dragon Colony of artists, musicians, and actors in the 1890s; Ellen and Eliza Virginia Scripps, the half-sisters whose philanthropic efforts created buildings and institutions that grew into important historic landmarks; and Walter Lieber, one of the first businessmen in La Jolla, who took a special interest in trees and parks.

INTRODUCTION

Long identified as "The Jewel," La Jolla has always been an extraordinary place to live as well as to visit. The Mediterranean-like climate is idyllic. The topography—sandy beaches, incredible rock formations, mystical caves, high cliffs rising from the sea, ocean canyons running for miles, and steep hillsides affording fabulous views—attracted humankind from the very beginning. That beginning dates to some 10,000 years ago when nomadic hunters camped along the shoreline and in all probability enjoyed the same magnificent sunsets as La Jollans do today, with the sun an unbelievable orange-red fireball sinking in the blue waters of the Pacific. The great natural beauty blending sea, sky, and land in a fashion that is totally unique has always made La Jolla stand out among the myriad of Southern California beach towns up and down the coastline.

People began driving horses and carriages to La Jolla from the boomtown of San Diego to enjoy its beauties in the mid-to-late 19th century. At low tide, they collected mosses and shells. They picnicked on barren beaches. They photographed themselves staunchly arranged on or beside stupendous natural formations left by the waves of time: Alligator Head, Cathedral Rock, Goldfish Point, and the "White Lady" cave. A newspaper journal of 1869 records the experience:

> Had the pleasure of a ride to this noted place on Sunday last. Every person having any poetry in his soul, or an eye for the beautiful and grand in nature should make a pilgrimage to this place. The deep caverns in the rocks, the roar of the wild wave, the sea mosses to be gathered all go to make this one of the most desirable places to visit about San Diego.

Sooner rather than later, La Jolla had permanent residents. In 1887, Frank Terrell Botsford, a stockbroker from New York, purchased 400 acres and set up the first La Jolla Park subdivision. He formed a partnership with another native easterner, George Webster Heald, and the two of them laid out plans for the seaside village and immediate residential area we know today. Heald himself bought three acres in La Jolla Park, built a barn in which to reside at first (he highly prized his horses), and then erected a Victorian-style farmhouse.

Although the attractions of La Jolla were many, early residents suffered from a continuing dilemma: the lack of fresh water. In auctioning the first lots on April 30, 1887, Botsford had grandiosely promised that springs were nearby, but they were really located over a mountain, from which water had to be brought in by horse and wagon. He had also promised a railway connection, but that was some time in coming. In the spirit of the 1880s boomtown developers, Botsford further noted that a grand-scale hotel would take shape, an act that did not happen until the next decade. Still, by the start of the 20th century, La Jolla had about 200 residents—some among them rich and famous—coping in the frontier spirit of dirt roads, oil and candle lanterns, a sparse water supply (it was a three bathtub town!), no plumbing, and cows straying on the beaches.

About 100 wooden cottages were built along the ocean hillsides, mostly small in scale except for one grand Victorian surrounded by gardens on the oceanfront. Built in 1896, South Moulton Villa was named after a street in London and belonged to Ellen Browning Scripps, the newspaper heiress whose philanthropies and cultural and educational gifts to La Jolla were to vastly change the community over the next 30 years.

Another endearing female figure in La Jolla's history rose to prominence in the 1890s. She was German-born Anna Held, who had come to this country as a kindergarten teacher, served as a nanny to the children of Ulysses S. Grant, and arrived by horse and buggy to see La Jolla one day and promptly purchased ocean hillside property. She built her own home and attracted an international following of musicians, artists, writers, and teachers that would become the highly revered Green Dragon Colony. They were housed in a dozen artistically—and at times eccentrically—shaped cottages overlooking the sea.

Unique to early La Jolla history is how the first cottages in the Green Dragon as well as elsewhere were known by whimsical names instead of street addresses. Some examples are the Ark (shaped like a boat), the Dreamery (with two sleeping towers), Columbine (flowers), Wisteria (with a vine-covered pergola), and any number of the usual appellations denoting sleepy, cozy places such as Nestledown, Tuckaway, and Breezy Nest. Many of the cottages were built as beach rentals by pioneer citizens such as Anson and Nellie Mills and Walter Lieber.

The 1920s were important and extremely prosperous years for La Jolla, enticing wealthy citizens from around the world to establish residences in the village by the sea that was becoming more and more attractive after the addition of cultural and educational facilities funded mainly by Ellen Browning Scripps. During these years, too, La Jolla established its reputation as a resort community with the opening of two posh hotels: the La Valencia and the Casa de Mañana. A pair of social institutions—the La Jolla Country Club and the La Jolla Beach and Yacht (now Tennis) Club—also took shape, along with the establishment of Girard Avenue as a fashionable street of shops where fancy jewelers rubbed elbows with equally fancy grocers. Three new La Jolla subdivisions were laid out as locations for opulent estates and villas: the Muirlands, on a hillside high above the ocean with fantastic sea vistas; La Jolla Shores, located near warm, sandy beaches; and La Jolla Hermosa, desirable because of its proximity to the electric railroad running from San Diego. Homes for the sites were designed by such architects as William Templeton Johnson, Edgar Ullrich, and Thomas Shepherd, who set the tone for the historic Spanish Revival (sometimes eclectically combined with English Tudor and Cape Cod) style that characterizes La Jolla architecture today.

Though slower in growth, the 1930s and 1940s offered several notable changes. A major transportation artery—Torrey Pines Road—made La Jolla more accessible by automobiles than any previous time in history. The Children's Pool was dedicated as a community location for ocean access without danger. In 1941, clouds of war gathered, and the federal government erected Camp Callan as a military base only a few miles north of the village. La Jolla, "The Jewel," still shone brightly, but the imminent threat of World War II would change the easygoing life of its inhabitants forever.

One

THE ENCHANTING SEA

The incredible beauty of natural wonders—the amazing blue Pacific bordered by high, jagged sandstone cliffs and unusual rock formations created over eons of time—brought the first visitors to La Jolla in the mid-to-late 19th century. They were astounded by beach formations such as Alligator Head, an immense crocodilian stone clump rising out of the water like some prehistoric sea monster as waves crashed around it. Equally enchanting were formations such as Cathedral Rock, which sat on the shoreline soaring skyward with a Queen Victoria silhouette carved out in the middle, and the famous White Lady cave—eminently mysterious, eerie, and romantic.

"Would you like to see the most beautiful coast scenery in California?" asked a railroad advertisement for travel to La Jolla in the 1880s. After the first tracks were laid in 1885, trains left daily from San Diego to La Jolla and back. Round-trips, at 75¢, allowed visitors to see the sights and visit the beaches. Excursions were always most popular at low tide, when beautiful mosses and shells could be collected along the shoreline and lazy garibaldi could be seen sunning themselves off the promontory known as Goldfish Point. La Jolla's Seven Caves in a Row were also accessible during low tide. Located under ocean cliffs more than 100 feet high, they were a spectacle unto themselves. In 1902, the cave named Sunny Jim (after a comic strip character of the time) was dug out and made reachable via 133 stairway steps by entrepreneur tourist Prof. Gustav Schulz. Like many people who came to La Jolla in its early days, Professor Schulz was sold on its incredible natural wonders as a sure draw for visitors—and the soon-to-come parade of permanent settlers as the century progressed.

Within the photo: THE COVE (About 1897)   Brockton Villa   Green Dragon   The Breakers

LA JOLLA COVE, 1890s. The sea and its many enchantments lured the first visitors to La Jolla. They found a rugged coastline that boasted to be "the most beautiful" in California and, more specifically, a lovely, protected cove that was popular for bathing and picnicking. Some tourists arrived by horse-drawn buggies, but in 1885, railroad tracks were laid for round-trip travel from San Diego to La Jolla. The first beach cottages were built along the barren cliffs above the cove in the 1890s.

ALLIGATOR HEAD, 1899. Dramatic rock formations carved over time were an early La Jolla tourist attraction. This one became popularly known as Alligator Head because of its resemblance to the animal's broad snout. Located at La Jolla Cove, it was for many years a focal point for photographs and tourist postcards. Crashing waves gradually eroded the formation over the decades, and the last part disappeared into the ocean in a winter storm during the 1970s.

CATHEDRAL ROCK, 1905. The dawn of the 20th century found visitors to La Jolla marveling over Queen Victoria's silhouette, apparent in this ocean-side wonder rising in the sky with a jagged spire resembling a European cathedral. The various earth and sea movements that created it over thousands of years remain a mystery. History records, however, that the rock disappeared during a severe winter storm in the early morning hours of January 19, 1906. It is now lost but for a few old photographs.

THE WHITE LADY. One of the most renowned and dramatically photographed attractions in early La Jolla history was the White Lady cave. When visitors view it from inside looking toward the ocean, they see a white lady's silhouette. Legend has it that a newly wedded bride was once trapped in the cave and was swallowed by the ocean. In 1904, Rose Hartwick Thorpe immortalized the legend in her book *The White Lady of La Jolla*: "She is robed in shimmering garments of light, wrapped in a misty veil, and on her head is a wreath like a coronet of orange blossoms."

SEVEN CAVES, 1909. Deep, mysterious caves, first explored thousands of years ago by Native Americans, beneath high ocean cliffs and all located in a row, have astounded scientists and the general public alike from the earliest of times. The San Diego–La Jolla Railway Company built a flight of stairs to access the caves from above the cliff in 1899, and they soon became popular attractions. A private entrepreneur named Prof. Gustav Schulz also dug a tunnel to access one of the caves in 1902, complete with 133 steps.

THE CAVEMEN, 1917. As a prominent part of La Jolla history, the caves led to the formation of an organization called the Cavemen, which met on a regular basis. Members maintained that "the caves of La Jolla are to the California sea coast what the giant redwoods are to the Yosemite." Those applying for membership were asked to sign with their own blood. Prominent among them were J. C. Harper, attorney to Ellen Browning Scripps; and Dr. William Ritter, head of the Scripps Institution of Oceanography.

EMERALD COVE. The beautiful blue-green of the water encouraged the name of a small cove located a short distance from the greater La Jolla Cove. It was designated Emerald Cove. Good swimmers in the right tidal conditions could swim to the far side, where many golden-colored garibaldis could often be found lazily sunning themselves. These fish led to the name of the topside cliffs above—Goldfish Point, still a popular La Jolla tourist attraction.

DEVIL'S SLIDE, 1904. This deep ravine, barely accessible to humans and dropping to the ocean, was deemed the Devil's Slide early in La Jolla's history. It took "almost as long to do the descent as Milton gave Lucifer to reach the nether world," and "the upgrade pull was like the majority of the evil one's ways, hard to get away from," according to a *San Diego Union* newspaper article of March 5, 1899. Construction of a wooden stair made coming and going easier, but the name remained unchanged.

COVE PICNIC, 1910. La Jolla Cove became an idyllic destination for beach picnics even before any permanent homes were built in the area or a single railway line brought visitors to see the sights along the ocean. Horse-drawn wagons and carriages from San Diego carried many early sightseers. In this photograph, a finely dressed group of Sunday school children enjoys a small cove party with parents and teachers. There is no sure evidence of how they arrived at the cove, though the date suggests the rail line would have been available.

BY THESE ROCKS. At the start of the 20th century, more and more visitors were becoming interested in "beautiful La Jolla by the sea." Many old black-and-white photographs were taken around the ever-alluring rock formations along the beach—not only the famous ones such as Alligator Head and Cathedral Rock, but lesser stone works of nature such as these. In the below image, a family has gathered in 1902; above, two children playfully pose around a hole in a rock at an undated (though probably similar) time.

SEA FINDS. The Pacific Ocean—on La Jolla's west side—yielded a plenitude of exotic mosses, shells, and marine life that appealed to those going on collecting expeditions in the late 19th and early 20th centuries. Charles Darwin's *The Origin of Species* continued to intrigue many, and the Victorian era's fascination for collecting striking and unusual ephemera from nature ran rampant among those privileged to visit interesting places. This group's sea outing on Long Beach (later renamed La Jolla Shores) was obviously successful.

COWS AT THE BEACH, 1906. La Jolla Shores became one of La Jolla's best-known resort beaches, a pristine stretch of white sand beautifully manicured and filled with sunbathers. At the beginning of the 20th century, however, the beach sometimes proved an enjoyable place for the Holstein cows that were part of a nearby Long Beach dairy run for many years by the family of early resident Jeremiah Lee Holliday. In pioneer days, the Shores were also used for farmland. Among the crops grown were lima beans and grapes.

SEA SPLASHING. A good time awaited all those who came to be by La Jolla's beautiful sea. Bathing suits soon became the fashion of the day, worn not only for fun in the ocean, but also on the streets. In June 1917, a bathing suit ordinance was adopted to keep suited bathers in the vicinity of La Jolla Cove "unless there is worn over . . . a coat, cloak or other garment covering the entire person except head, hands and feet." Punishment was a $25 fine or 25-day jail sentence. The swimmers in these photographs, both above and below, are in compliance.

WHALE OF A TIME, 1903. Residents and sightseers from miles around turned out in full dress when this behemoth washed ashore at Long Beach (La Jolla Shores) in 1903. Whales occasionally beached themselves or encountered small boats that hindered their swimming along the shore and southward migration. And sometimes they were actually hunted for meat. Infamous to La Jolla history, a whale barbecue was held at the cove in 1917, complete with a 45-piece band. Hundreds attended the event.

THE BIG JUMP. Daredevil Horace Poole made several dangerous but successful dives from a springboard placed over the caves in 1897–1898 as entertainment for sightseers. His dive on July 4, 1898, was especially spectacular, as he covered his body with oil and set himself afire like a whirling dervish on the way down before splashing into the ocean. Poole also performed daredevil dives in other locations around San Diego, including one from a plane in Ocean Beach. Retired from diving, he died peacefully at his home in San Diego in 1943.

FIRST BATHHOUSE, 1894. The ever-attractive La Jolla Cove was the site of the first bathhouse, erected in 1894 by the railroad company. The small wooden structure offered coffee and cold drinks to visitors who came to La Jolla from San Diego by rail to enjoy a day at the beach. This photograph shows the first bathhouse shortly before it was remodeled to provide extended facilities and a more picturesque profile.

FIRST BATHHOUSE, AFTER REMODELING. A new roof and a coat of paint improved the bathhouse later in 1904. Sturdy wooden stairs allowed access to the La Jolla Cove beach, and swings were erected for further recreation. A small group of boats awaited those who wished to row offshore. Unfortunately, the bathhouse burned to the ground within a half-hour after a gasoline stove exploded on August 28, 1905, while the manager was cooking.

NEW BATHHOUSE, 1906. Much larger and imposing for its time, the second bathhouse opened on the same site in March 1906. It contained an auditorium, a swimming pool that was later floored and turned into a dance hall, and a restaurant overlooking the cove. The only facility at the time available for social life and recreation, it became the pride of the small La Jolla community. For the increasing groups of tourists coming to La Jolla for a one-day holiday, it offered 180 dressing rooms and lockers.

NEW BATHHOUSE. By the summer of 1906, the new bathhouse was in full swing, pervaded by a Coney Island atmosphere. Spring water, saltwater baths, and even clothing were promoted by advertising on the facade. The café was filled with people, while the beach served as a playground for bathers. All was well until 1922, when the commercial atmosphere began to disturb village inhabitants, who demanded its demolition. Controversy continued over the bathhouse until 1924, when it was finally torn down with no proposals for erecting another.

SURF'S UP, EARLY 1900S. The winter months in La Jolla offered one of the most beautiful surf scenes in California as storm waves crashed against the beach. The air was crisp, and the froth of the waves spewed against the rocks with the romance of a Shelley or Lord Byron poem. In this Kodak black-and-white photograph of 1906, one such spectacular wave crashes onto Alligator Head at La Jolla Cove. While early summers brought tourists and visitors, the winters were alive with their own sense of spirit and nature in its purest forms.

SUNSET, EARLY 1900. La Jolla was never lovelier than at a sunset, when the gold and purple colors of the sky melded with the glassy reflections in the blue Pacific. The few sparse inhabitants of La Jolla—about 100 in number, living in mostly self-built wooden houses along dirt paths for streets—took time out and paused in wonder at the place they inhabited. Early La Jolla realtor Walter Lieber even acknowledged the beauty of the sunsets in the telephone number for his beach rentals: Sunset 91.

Two

EARLY PIONEERS

The people were connected by dirt paths that ran from house to house, strung along the high cliffs overlooking the beautiful blue waters of the Pacific. At night, they carried little lanterns, lighting the way like so many fireflies. Their lives were simple—a card game here and there, a family dinner with friends or a big night out for a silent movie, a whirl on the dance pavilion, or a literary reading.

In 1900, La Jolla had only 200 residents, who lived mainly in small cottages and depended on supplies brought by horse and wagon from downtown San Diego. Although they were pioneers in the true sense, a certain cultural sensibility seemed to separate them from the usual migratory population that settled the American West. One of their first buildings was not the customary town hall but rather a very civilized library, appointed by intellectual books of the time and a finely tuned piano.

Who were La Jolla's pioneers? Founder Frank Botsford had been a New York stockbroker. Anson Mills was a well-educated New Englander of Maine ancestry. Anna Held came from Germany with a love for theater and music. Walter Lieber's past included an old, well-established Philadelphia family. Ellen Browning Scripps had retired from a lucrative newspaper business and started a new career devoted to education, culture, and philanthropy.

Whatever their past, La Jolla's early citizens seemed to realize they inhabited a special place in the world where the cultivation of one's mind was as important as the daily routine of living. They loved their "beautiful La Jolla by the sea" and determined to do their best to add to the natural setting with artistically designed buildings and parks.

In the early 1880s, Ellen Morrill Mills wrote in her remembrances, "La Jolla was just a beautiful expanse of gray-green sage brush and darker chaparral with patches of brilliant wildflowers here and there from the top of Mt. Soledad to the cove." The pioneers had arrived to change that, but never to forget the essence of La Jolla.

FRANK TERRELL BOTSFORD, C. 1870.
Known as the Father of La Jolla, Botsford first glimpsed the location in March 1886 and immediately became interested in development potential. He was born in Michigan and lived in many parts of the country before becoming a New York City stockbroker who made sufficient money to "buy La Jolla." The price for the 400 acres along the ocean identified as La Jolla Park was $5.50 an acre. The first lots were sold at a large public auction on April 30, 1887, and other sales continued at a brisk pace until a land crash in 1888.

CAMPING OUT, 1887. Botsford envisioned La Jolla as an Elysian setting with homes idyllically set along the cliffs and beaches. In the early days, he often camped, hunted game, and fished in the area. One of his continuing quests was to locate fresh springs that would provide water for the residents of the community, since the desert-like environment by the sea had access only to saltwater. The quest was unsuccessful for years, and water had to be brought by horse and wagon from several miles away.

ANNA HELD, C. 1890S. A person of tremendous spirit, humor, and determination, Held came to La Jolla in 1894, purchased a lot with an ocean view for $165, and started an internationally recognized colony of artists, musicians, writers, and actors that became known as the Green Dragon. Born in Berlin in 1849, Held had crossed the ocean to become the first kindergarten teacher in the United States. She served as a nanny to the children of Ulysses S. Grant II, and it was the Grants who introduced her to La Jolla when they were in San Diego. She is known as one of the first to bring cultural and social life to the village.

SUMMERTIME, 1890S. During the creation of the Green Dragon Colony—from 1894 until she sold it in 1912 for $30,000—Held met the great love of her life in musician Max Heinrich. They are photographed here in their summer house, built as part of the property. Heinrich died on a concert tour shortly after the marriage. Held later moved to London and died in 1942 at age 93. She had crossed the ocean 44 times and led a full, if sometime tumultuous, life.

THE GREEN DRAGON, 1898. Held's house was the center of life at the Green Dragon, which eventually grew to a dozen cottages perched along the beach cliffs, including one eccentrically shaped dwelling known as Noah's Ark. Daily life was devoted to music concerts, literary readings, and other cultural pursuits, as well as practical activities such as watering the garden and doing the laundry. Architect Irving Gill designed Held's cottage after she built the fireplace.

ANSON PEASLEE MILLS, C. 1900. The son of many generations of old New Englanders, Mills was born in Augusta, Maine, and graduated from Kents Hill as an attorney to be admitted to the Maine bar before he was even 21. He did not practice for long, however, and soon became one of the many young men seeking their fortunes by traveling West. He landed in La Jolla with his wife, Eleanor (familiarly "Nellie"), and spent many years as a pioneer community figure. He is best known for his daily journals of life in La Jolla. Called *The Mills Diaries*, they run from 1898 to 1932.

MILLS FAMILY, 1890S. Members of the Mills family from Maine often gathered in La Jolla, and several became permanent residents. Anson and Nellie's daughter Ellen, who had literary aspirations, wrote for the *La Jolla Journal* newspaper and published poetry. She also served as the *Journal*'s city editor for about 15 years. Nellie's sister Olivia Mudgett moved to La Jolla in the 1890s and started one of the town's first real estate businesses. Mudgett and the Mills family built two well-known early La Jolla homes: Kennebec and Villa Waldo.

WHEELER BAILEY, C. 1900. Coming to San Diego in 1886, Bailey (right) began a brick and tile business, providing many of the building materials for the Hotel del Coronado and later the 1915–1916 California Exposition in Balboa Park. In 1907, he commissioned architects Irving Gill and Frank Mead to construct a weekend retreat in La Jolla. Bailey's house became a social gathering spot for many cultural events during early decades of the community. Bailey sat on several fine arts boards and served as secretary-treasurer of the Bishop's School. He left a large estate upon his death in 1935.

WHEELER BAILEY HOUSE, 1907. Noted for its bold architecture and extraordinary setting on a rocky beachside promontory, the Bailey House attracted international attention for its design. It was in keeping with Irving Gill's philosophy: "We should build our house simple, plain and substantial as a boulder, then leave the ornamentation to Nature, who will tone it with lichens, chisel it with storms." The house faces out on two magnificent La Jolla views. The high cliffs and mystical caves are to the left, and straight ahead are the peaceful yet sometimes ebullient waters of the cove. Remaining today, it is a designated historic landmark.

W. F. LUDINGTON, 1897. Known as La Jolla's original businessman, Ludington took charge of the first general merchandise store, which had been started a short time before by his father-in-law, George W. Chase. Active in community affairs, Ludington served in the California Legislature in 1908. He also held offices in numerous other organizations in San Diego and La Jolla, including the Cuyamaca Club and the La Jolla Country Club. Ludington Heights, the residential neighborhood above Torrey Pines Road, where he built two of his own homes, is named for him.

GEORGE W. CHASE, C. 1900. Leaving New England in 1880, Chase brought his family across the country by covered wagon. They arrived first in National City and then moved to La Jolla, where Chase erected a store out of adobe brick near the cove. After Chase's daughter married W. F. Ludington, the store operated as Chase and Ludington and was a business fixture in the early days of La Jolla. Most staples were brought by wagon from San Diego twice a week.

CHARLIE THE CHINAMAN, 1917. Eccentric characters were common along the dusty streets of the seaside village. Among them was Charlie, who raised vegetables and peddled them with horse and wagon around town. He knew each customer by name and always greeted them with "howdy do, Missy." Well-liked by everyone, he loved motion pictures and had his own seat at La Jolla's most popular movie palace. Misfortune befell Charlie when he was arrested for possessing an opium pipe, but local citizenry was happy to bail him out of jail. He returned to China in 1924.

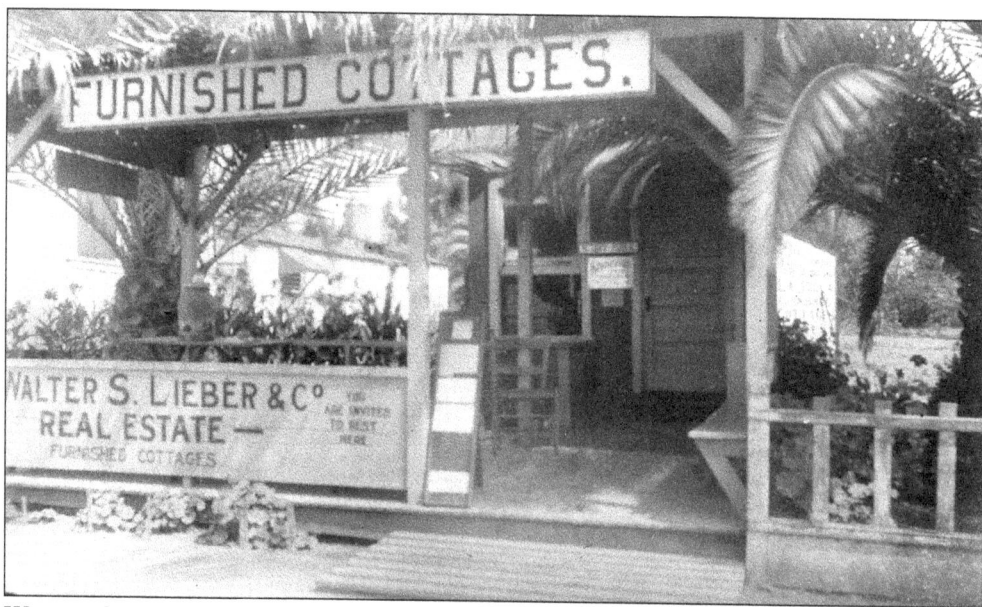

WALTER SCOTT LIEBER REAL ESTATE, C. 1905. Raised in a wealthy Philadelphia family, Lieber started in the mining business but came to La Jolla in 1904 after the high altitudes of mining country became disagreeable to his health. He built and rented beach cottages and developed philanthropies for many years, as well as devoting efforts to culture and the parklands in early La Jolla, which he poetically referred to as "beautiful La Jolla by the sea." He was remembered as one of the town's most-loved first citizens upon his death in 1945.

FLORENCE SAWYER, C. 1890S. Sawyer was a guest at the La Jolla Park Hotel in 1895, when it was brought to her attention that La Jolla needed a library. She bought and donated a lot for the site at Girard and Wall Streets, hired builders for construction, and purchased furnishings before capping the effort with a $1,000 donation in books. Sawyer's aid to La Jolla was extraordinary, but her time in the town was brief. In 1899, she married John Ransome Riley in Los Angeles.

THE READING ROOM, 1897. With its slight touch of Victorian bric-a-brac and decorative relief work, the Reading Room was an endearing addition to a village that, at the time, was trying to grow out of a dusty town at the end of a rail line. It was used for literary readings and, along with the bathhouse at the cove, was one of the few places for residents to gather for social and cultural events. Tastefully chosen by Florence Sawyer, the furnishings included wood tables and chairs clustered around a fireplace and a piano.

JOSEPHINE SEAMAN. Born in London in 1912, Seaman spent her early life engaged in missionary work. She traveled to India and lived in China for many years before coming in 1921 to La Jolla, where she spent the rest of her long life devoted to philanthropies and good works through a variety of cultural, social, and educational institutions. Seaman was known throughout California for championing women's rights and proved a dynamic speaker on the subject before many clubs and organizations.

CAREY CREST. Seaman's home, high on an ocean cliff with magnificent views, was a landmark in the La Jolla community and a social gathering place on many occasions. It was originally built in 1890 as a residence for Joseph and Hettie Carey. Seaman purchased the house in 1921 and lived there until her death in 1958, becoming the owner most identified with the Craftsman structure. She developed seaside hilltop gardens, which were meticulously kept for many years by her British gardener.

HOUSE OF DREAMS, C. 1910. An international traveler, collector, and antiquarian, Florence Palmer came to La Jolla in 1905 and built one of the town's most extraordinary early residences, combining elements of Japanese design with traditional California Craftsman architecture. She filled her House of Dreams with exotic tapestries and antiques. Extensive gardens, developed in the Japanese style, included more than 300 trees and a teahouse.

Three

THE SCRIPPS LEGACY

One name seldom means so much to a community as "Scripps" does to La Jolla. The family behind the name bequeathed to the place practically all things connected to beauty and greatness: art centers, cultural facilities, schools, hospitals, playgrounds, parks, scientific institutions, and churches. Without Ellen Browning Scripps—the quiet one—and her half-sister Eliza Virginia Scripps—the noisy one—La Jolla would never have been what it was then, is now, or will be in the future.

Ellen Browning and Eliza Virginia arrived in 1896, both wealthy from newspaper fortunes. Both also had generous hearts for philanthropy and over the next decades endowed numerous La Jolla undertakings. The La Jolla Recreation Center, the Bishop's School, the Scripps Hospital, the La Jolla Woman's Club, the Scripps Institution of Oceanography, Scripps Park, the Children's Pool, and St. James-by-the-Sea Episcopal Church—all major La Jolla landmarks—are primary examples.

Ellen Browning operated from an impressive seaside home overlooking the Pacific with park-like gardens she often invited the public to visit. Eliza Virginia also owned property in La Jolla, including Wisteria Cottage, now part of the La Jolla Historical Society's headquarters, but was generally a more wayward figure and died on a world tour in London in 1921. Ellen Browning died at her La Jolla home in 1932. She was 96, by far the most revered figure the community had ever known.

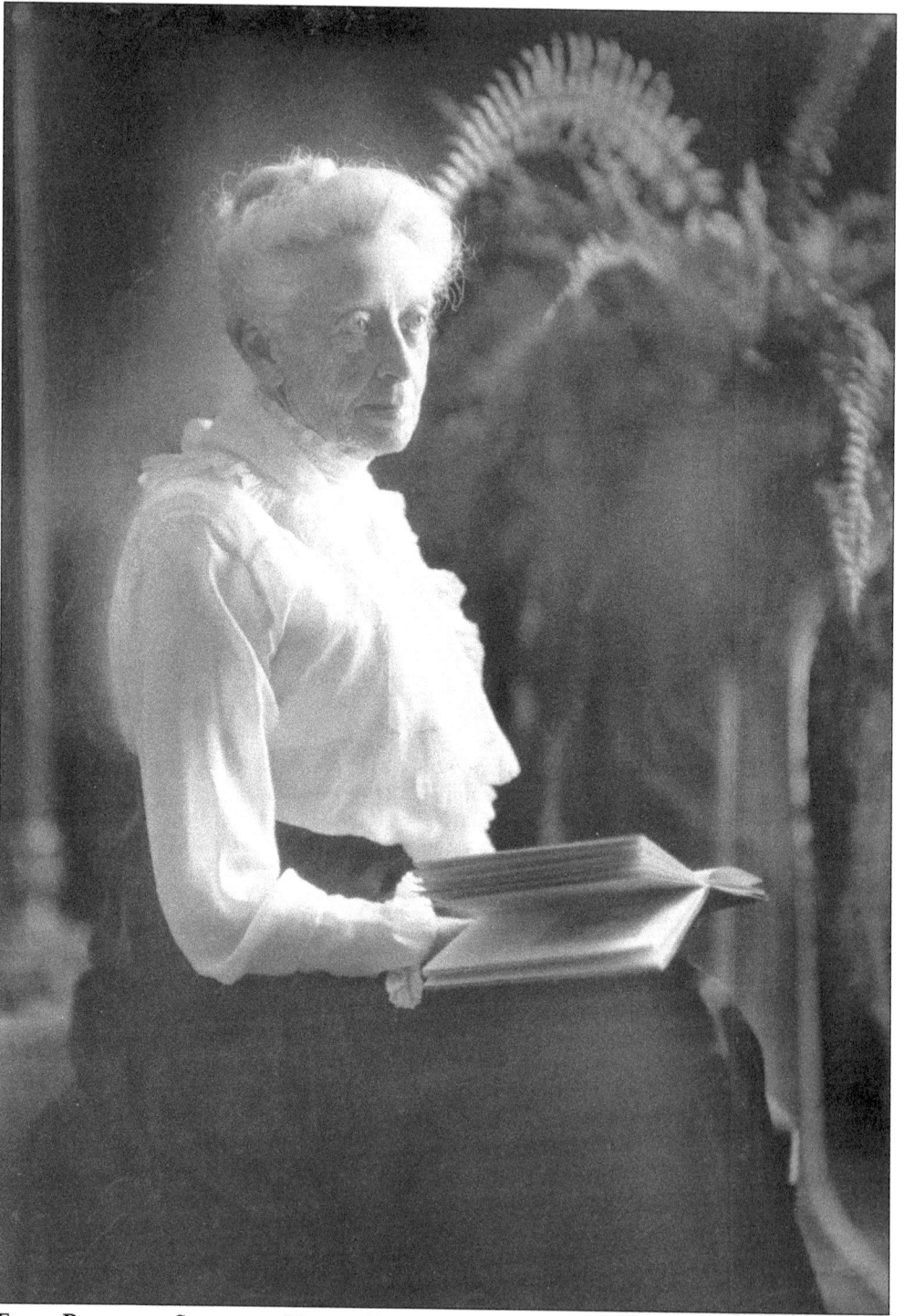

ELLEN BROWNING SCRIPPS AT HOME. Ellen Browning Scripps was 61 years old when she came to La Jolla to retire and build her home. She remained in La Jolla and devoted a lifetime to various philanthropies in the community. Living a simple and frugal life, she was known for independent thinking despite having a somewhat demure personality.

ELLEN BROWNING SCRIPPS PORTRAIT. Born on South Moulton Street in the heart of London in 1836, Ellen Browning was the daughter of James Mogg Scripps, whose ancestry was connected to the philosopher John Locke. Her father immigrated to America in 1844, bringing his daughter and five other siblings to settle in Rushville, Illinois. Ellen Browning, a child of unusual intelligence, graduated from Knox College. She entered the newspaper business with her brother and accumulated a vast fortune.

ELIZA VIRGINIA SCRIPPS PORTRAIT. Born in London in 1852 and familiarly known as "Jenny," Eliza Virginia was also a philanthropist but is mostly remembered in La Jolla for her eccentric personality. She openly chastised people in the streets for littering, interrupted church sermons, and stopped trains whenever she felt like it. One of her great loves was the color purple, and she thought it was her privilege to be the only person in town to wear it.

ELIZA VIRGINIA SCRIPPS. An explorer and adventurer, Eliza Virginia Scripps could often be spotted riding horses around La Jolla or hiking up Mount Soledad to see what she could discover in natural fauna. She also collected seaweed and shells and decorated an entire room with it. Her love of adventure led to a world trip in 1920, during which she developed an illness that resulted in her death in London in 1921.

WISTERIA COTTAGE, EARLY 1900S. Eliza Virginia Scripps purchased Wisteria Cottage in La Jolla in the early 1900s. The previous owner had built the cottage near her half-sister's home in 1904. Eliza Virginia commissioned architect Irving Gill to redesign the house, which she then relinquished to the St. James-by-the-Sea Episcopal Church for temporary use. The cottage is now part of the La Jolla Historical Society facilities.

SOUTH MOULTON VILLA, 1899. Construction began on Ellen Browning Scripps's impressive Victorian-style house overlooking the ocean in 1896. It was completed a year later, and extensive gardens were soon planted to surround the property. The interior included a large library and one room decorated with shells and seaweed. The house burned in an arson fire in 1915.

SOUTH MOULTON VILLA, C. 1920. After the fire, Ellen Browning commissioned architect Irving Gill to design a much more modern house on the same site as the previous home. It was in keeping with Gill's new style of using tilt-up concrete walls and a flowing curved arch as the main entry. The same principles were applied to many Gill designs for the public buildings endowed by Ellen Browning Scripps in central La Jolla.

LATHE HOUSE, 1924. Built adjacent to the second Moulton Villa, the Lathe House complemented the modern architecture of Ellen Browning Scripps's residence. It was designed by the San Diego firm of Gardner and Slaymaker using redwood formed into geometric shapes to interplay with light and shadow. Interior details included Japanese elements and a tea room.

COMMUNITY HOUSE, 1915. Later renamed the La Jolla Recreation Center, this is one of Ellen Browning Scripps's first gifts to the community, featuring a playground for the children of La Jolla as well as a performance hall and meeting rooms. It was designed by architect Irving Gill using tilt-up concrete construction with a series of graceful arches celebrating the facade.

THE BISHOP'S SCHOOL, EARLY 1900S. The first buildings for the educational facility— initially exclusively for girls—were erected in 1909 and designed by architect Irving Gill on grounds donated by the Scripps family. A landmark tower was added in 1930 after a design by architect Carleton Winslow. Both the original architecture and landscape continue to be preserved.

LA JOLLA WOMAN'S CLUB, 1914. The organization held its first meeting in this clubhouse on October 5, 1914. Ellen Browning Scripps again played the fairy godmother, donating land, the building, and the Irving Gill design. The architecture is typical Gill of this period, as it makes generous use of arches and columns with tilt-up concrete forming the facade.

SCRIPPS PARK. Originally designated La Jolla Shoreline Park, the landmark location bordering La Jolla Cove was renamed in 1927 to honor the revered benefactress on her 91st birthday. The site had been home to two bathhouses at the start of the 20th century: the first built in 1894 and destroyed by fire in 1905, the second demolished in 1924 when it was considered an eyesore.

SCRIPPS INSTITUTION OF OCEANOGRAPHY. Ellen Browning Scripps promised Dr. William Ritter, head of the department of biology at the University of California, that if he would locate in La Jolla, she would provide a building for scientific work devoted to marine life. The Scripps Institution was first built at La Jolla Cove in 1905, but two years later, the scientists moved what would soon become an internationally known facility to land farther north on the La Jolla shoreline.

SCRIPPS METABOLIC CLINIC, 1924. When Ellen Browning Scripps fell and broke her hip in 1922, she became convinced that La Jolla needed a larger hospital than the one that had been constructed in 1916. She donated funds for the new hospital. It became the basis for the world-renowned and multi-faceted Scripps Memorial Hospital Group, now located north of La Jolla.

43

CHILDREN'S POOL, 1931. As one of the last philanthropic efforts for the community before her death in 1932, Ellen Browning Scripps spearheaded a breakwater project to make a safer area for swimming on the La Jolla coastline. The 300-foot breakwater took more than a decade to complete, and the design was heralded as a feat of modern engineering.

ST. JAMES-BY-THE-SEA EPISCOPAL CHURCH, 1907. One of the oldest churches in La Jolla, St. James occupies land donated by both Ellen Browning and Eliza Virginia Scripps. The building was designed by architect Irving Gill. The tower was added later by Ellen Browning in memory of her half-sister after her death in 1921. It replicates a structure from a church in Campo Florida, Mexico.

TORREY PINES STATE PARK, 1908. Unusual maritime pines growing along the cliffs north of La Jolla came to the attention of scientists as early as the 1850s. In the late 19th century, they were named *Pinus torreyana* in honor of Dr. John Torrey, an eminent botanist. The trees were of great interest to Ellen Browning Scripps. In 1908, she purchased land on which they were growing and created a shoreline state park.

Four

CHURCHES, CULTURE, COMMERCE, AND SOCIAL LIFE

The magnificent sea cliffs, deep blue waters of the Pacific, and amenable climate soon made La Jolla a destination for residents and tourists alike. Churches, banks, and social and cultural institutions soon began to spring up in the village by the sea, along with an interesting array of commercial endeavors. Resort hotels were added to the mix in the 1920s, a prosperous time for all. La Jolla was seen to be "unique among the watering places of the southland shore: Tennis and golf, horseback riding and motoring into San Diego's interesting back country, swimming and surf bathing are here provided for in a perfectly natural California way," according to one hotel promotion.

The romance of Spanish Revival architecture was felt with the addition of several major buildings, such as the Casa de Mañana, La Valencia Hotel, and the Athenaeum Art and Music Library. New social life came to town in the 1920s in the form of the La Jolla Beach and Yacht Club and the La Jolla Country Club. Banks, grocery stores, restaurants, and tea rooms brought amenities to mark La Jolla as a memorable place to live and to visit.

MARY, STAR OF THE SEA, 1909. The first Catholic church in La Jolla was a small, Gothic-inspired wooden structure named after the blessed mother and completed in 1909. It was built by the pastor, Fr. Joseph Mesny, with the help of a carpenter on three lots at the corner of Girard and Kline Streets. The building served the congregation until plans for a new church began in 1935 with a Spanish-style design by architect Carlton Monroe Winslow.

ST. JAMES-BY-THE-SEA EPISCOPAL CHURCH, 1907. The oldest formal church established in La Jolla was this Episcopal church, designed in the Spanish style by architect Irving Gill. Gill was commissioned by Ellen Browning Scripps and her half-sister, Eliza Virginia Scripps. He designed many buildings in La Jolla for the Scripps sisters and their various civic philanthropies.

48

THE ATHENAEUM MUSEUM AND ARTS LIBRARY, 1921. The library dates to 1894, when a small organization of La Jollans formed a reading group. Members incorporated as the Library Association of La Jolla in 1899 and occupied a small building at the corner of Wall and Girard Streets known as the Reading Room. In 1921, architect William Templeton Johnson was commissioned to design this new structure for the library in a Spanish Revival style.

SWINGING TIME, C. 1900. Golf was a popular sport in early La Jolla, with several courses available for playing around the village and beaches. In 1913, the first major course was laid out on hills above the town, and the La Jolla Country Club was built as the focal point in 1927. Bylaws for the club were incorporated that same year with the idea of cultivating sports, particularly golf and tennis.

PAR FOR THE COURSE, 1915. Maintenance of the grounds for the La Jolla Country Club required much time and effort in the early days. The scarce water barely kept the grass growing in the desert-like environment, where even drinking water had to be brought into town by horse and wagon. But sport was important, and so the links were maintained. Here Taylor Rutherford is mowing in 1915.

LA JOLLA BEACH AND YACHT CLUB, 1927. Inspired by Mayan architecture, the club opened its doors in 1927 on the sandy beaches of La Jolla Shores. It offered "a safe harbor for boats" and many amenities, including a distinctively appointed lounge and dining room as well as a golf course and horses for riding. The name was later changed to the La Jolla Beach and Tennis Club.

SOCIAL WHIRL, C. 1930. The beach and yacht club was a popular gathering spot for many social occasions after it opened in the 1920s. Hollywood personalities joined the natives for beach parties, recreational sports, and an opportunity to collect local gossip. As popularity increased, new additions were constructed, although the yacht harbor envisioned in the original plan never really took shape.

LA VALENCIA, 1926. Spanish names continued to inspire 1920s-era hotels in La Jolla, with this one originally opened as a fine apartment hotel named Los Apartmentos de Sevilla with a "smart tea room, patio terraced gardens, and a spacious Spanish lobby." The name was shortened to La Valencia when the signature pink stucco tower with sparkling tiles was completed. Architect Reginald Johnson designed the hotel to take advantage of magnificent ocean views. It was built at a cost of $200,000.

CASA DE MAÑANA, 1924. A wealthy Colorado lady visiting La Jolla had a vision to build a first-class resort hotel by the blue Pacific. She purchased land and brought architect Edgar Ullrich to La Jolla from Colorado Springs to design the Spanish-inspired structure that would become the landmark House of Tomorrow. It was built around a beautifully landscaped court and contained a ballroom and lounge in the grand tradition.

COLONIAL, 1928. The description "touches of carving and gilding and graceful colonial stairways" graced advertisements for this imposing four-story apartment hotel, built in 1928 after a design by architect Frank Stevenson. It replaced an older hotel on Prospect that was actually moved to the back of the new building and operated as part of the general facility. The Colonial has had several names through its history and is now known as the Grande Colonial, La Jolla.

WESTERN UNION, 1921. The Western Union telegram office on Girard Street was the hub of communication in early La Jolla, where delivery boy Robert Wilson (left foreground) kept a busy schedule, coming and going on his bicycle, carrying news to citizens around the village. Wilson kept a little brown book with up-to-date listings of names and addresses to aid in his job.

CHASE AND LUDINGTON, 1890s. The first merchants in La Jolla were George W. Chase and William French Ludington, who operated this general store at the corner of Prospect and Girard Streets. A second story was added in 1902, giving the building one of the town's premium ocean views. La Jolla had very few stores in its early days, as most supplies arrived by horse and wagon from downtown San Diego.

COZENS GROCERY, C. 1920. A number of grocery stores began to operate on Girard in the second decade of the 20th century. Among them was Cozens, which had its own butcher and delivery man. Fresh produce and canned goods were provided for customers (note the neat triangular stacks of canned merchandise behind the counter). A bench offered an invitation to linger and gossip.

BARNES AND CALLOWAY, 1919. An imposing two-story commercial building was erected on Girard Street at the beginning of the profitable 1920s. It housed a grocery store owned by Barnes and Calloway, as well as the main post office. The La Jolla Brotherhood met upstairs. To the left of the building was the home of Dr. Martha Dunn Corey, a much-loved and respected La Jolla physician.

WHITE RABBIT ROOF GARDEN, 1917. Lewis Carroll's *Alice in Wonderland* inspired the opening of La Jolla's first roof restaurant in 1917. It offered ice cream, sodas, candy, and cigars to be enjoyed along with a fabulous view of the Pacific from a roof lightly shaded by palm fronds and a lath structure.

LA JOLLA BAKERY, 1910. Caleniero Torrini, an American of Italian origin, started the first bakery in 1903. His success resulted in the addition of a new front to enlarge the building in 1910. Another addition was built in 1928. Notice the unusual chimney to accommodate the ovens.

56

SMITH'S STORE, 1917. Smith's Store was a major shopping emporium of the early 20th century, offering a cornucopia of clothing ranging from the important white handkerchief to shoes, stockings, and household bric-a-brac. The store was located at 1049 Wall Street.

SOUTHERN TRUST AND SAVINGS BANK. Banking history began in La Jolla in 1907 with the establishment of Southern Trust and Savings at Girard and Prospect Streets. Southern Trust originally started in a less formal building but opened this more imposing structure at the same location in 1916, with a celebration including music and fruit punch. The institution later sold to the Bank of Italy, which subsequently became Bank of America.

INTERIOR, SOUTHERN TRUST, 1916. Banks of the early 1900s were noted for their marble interiors and references to historical decorative detail. Southern Trust had a white marble interior and a mosaic tile floor with a Greek key detail.

INTERIOR, U.S. NATIONAL BANK, 1924. Marble also decorated the U.S. National Bank, which opened its offices at Girard and Wall Streets in 1924. The same building also housed the Granada Theater, La Jolla's first and only old movie palace.

Five

RAILROADS AND
TRANSPORTATION

Horses, wagons, bicycles, and an indefatigable donkey named Rags provided early means of transport around the small seaside village, which was connected only by dirt paths prior to 1915. Visitors arrived by railroad from San Diego starting in 1894. By the beginning of the 20th century, the rail service offered a fancy gasoline-powered engine called the *Red Devil* for a swift and sleek ride between La Jolla and the larger metropolis.

Although the first automobile was seen in La Jolla in 1903 (owned by a British royal visiting the Green Dragon Colony), use of the car as a major means of transportation did not begin until about 15 years later. Like all other towns across the country, the arrival of the automobile changed the landscape considerably. Dirt paths that led along the beaches became streets and sidewalks with concrete pavement. Gas and service stations became part of the commercial core along Girard and Prospect Streets, along with car dealerships showcasing the latest in "swift motors." Other businesses offered the services of horse and wagons to hoist the automobiles out of ditches when they flipped over or slid into muddy ocean canyons during winter rainstorms.

Travel to and around La Jolla remained for the most part grounded, yet the ocean air currents offered the thrill of drifting in the skies, and the surf, of course, provided the adventure of riding the waves. Anne Lindberg, the wife of Charles Lindberg, launched a sailplane with a 60-foot wingspan from the top of Mount Soledad in 1930. Serious surfing began at La Jolla's Windansea Beach during that time as well. Although skiffs and boats were popularly seen around La Jolla beaches, they served mainly as pleasure craft rather than means of transport.

CAB SERVICE, C. 1900. Horse and wagon was the preferred and almost only way of getting around at the start of the 20th century. An early La Jolla entrepreneur named Frank Burnham put his mule and wagon into business as a cab service known as La Jolla Transfer. Not everyone living in town in the early 1900s kept his own horse and wagon, so Burnham's transportation service filled a niche, traveling the dirt paths to transport people between cottages and stores.

DONKEY-A-GO, 1907. In the early 1900s, a familiar donkey named Rags furnished communal transport around town, especially for children, who loved to sit in his cart and be pulled over the dirt pathways. Rags, who belonged to no one in particular, was always available for service to anyone who fed him. According to legend, one day, he broke into a keg of molasses behind a grocery store and became the sickest animal in town.

SADDLED UP, C. 1920S. The first concrete road in La Jolla was the Biological Grade, traveling north from the center of town and poured in 1915. Dirt roads in the village were not paved until three years later, so even though La Jolla had a few automobiles, horses were still a popular way to get around. Here Elizabeth Stevenson, a tourist from Connecticut, rides her mount to the new Southern Trust and Savings Bank.

FIRST AUTOMOBILE, 1902–1903. La Jolla's first car was owned by Lord Auberon Herbert (right), the son of Britain's third earl of Caernarvon, who came to La Jolla in the early 1900s to visit Anna Held's Green Dragon Colony. He enjoyed showing off his curious mechanical transport around town. Steered with a lever instead of a wheel, it once tipped over on Prospect Street after he offered a female passenger a ride and she accidentally fell on the lever.

SERVICE FOR WHEELS, C. 1915. As La Jolla's automobile population began to grow, businesses soon sprouted up along the streets to sell tires and gasoline as well as mechanical parts for repairs. Joy's Service Station was a popular spot that featured Red Crown gasoline at two drive-up pumps. The adjacent La Jolla Auto Service offered hand washes and grease jobs for the coveted flivvers. Bicycles were another means of early transport in La Jolla. Bicycles, which were repaired at the La Jolla Cyclery and Rushton's Bicycle Shop, provided one of the best ways of traveling the dirt paths and roadways in the early days before sidewalks and paved streets.

TAKING A SPIN, C. 1915. La Jolla residents Anson and Nellie Mills were among the first to own and operate an automobile. While enjoying a ride, they have parked for a photograph in front of the newly built Colonial Hotel. The Mills couple, a pioneer La Jolla family, contributed much to the community's social and cultural growth. Anson kept a series of journals recording daily life that provide an intimate look at history.

LITTLE ENGINE THAT COULD, 1894. On May 13, 1894, this engine pulled the first passenger cars into town. In the 1880s, the greatest drawback to the development (besides water) was the lack of transportation from San Diego. The arrival of the train changed that, and daily excursions were possible between the small beach village and the larger city. The engine was built in New York and shipped around the Horn.

TRAINLOAD, 1895. Crowds jammed both open and closed cars to come to La Jolla from San Diego via rails laid through Pacific Beach. Placards at the downtown San Diego station in the 1890s advertised La Jolla's low tides as the best times for visitors to explore tide pools, to collect shells and marine fossils, and to experience the awesome rock formations, cliffs, and caves along the beaches. Although many only came to visit, a good number of soon-to-be permanent residents also initially came by rail.

PEDAL TO THE METAL, C. 1900. The first engines that pulled railroad cars to La Jolla were engineered for short hauls, resulting in the train having to stop at intervals along the way to catch a breath. Consequently, the railroad company constantly upgraded engines to make the passage quick and pleasant. In 1894, the timetable listed the trip as an hour in length. In later years, it was reduced considerably—surprisingly to about the same as today's congested automobile commute!

FULL STEAM AHEAD, C. 1900. The traveler on a train to La Jolla enjoyed very different scenery than anyone traveling today. Open fields and empty hillsides filled the eyes through most of the commute, along with views of deserted sandy beaches. Occasional signs of civilization appeared in the form of an isolated farmhouse or communication lines.

TRAIN STOP, 1904. Compared to the elaborate train stations built in European cities, La Jolla's main station was an extremely simple affair—basically a small wooden barn on stilts and open at either end. It was located on Prospect Street near Fay Avenue, in close proximity to local hotels and the popular La Jolla Cove beaches and rock formations.

TRAIN WRECK, 1907. This wreck occurred when a car derailed near the Bishop's School, causing no known fatalities and few damages. But train wrecks between San Diego and La Jolla from the start of the railroad in 1894 to its demise in 1919 were sometimes severe, resulting in deaths and mangled wreckage. Spread rails were a common occurrence for derailment, along with the confrontation of a stray automobile or cow.

RED DEVIL, 1908. A fancy gasoline-driven engine and cars called the *Red Devil* also began to run between La Jolla and San Diego. It attracted many passengers who wanted to ride in class, dressed in their Sunday finery. The stop was at a small well-built little station that is still standing at Ivanhoe and Silverado Streets. Since the train had no accommodation to turn around, legend has it that it went up a slight hill and made a circle, hence the development of the Park Row circle drive.

ALL ABOARD, 1909. *Red Devil* conductor Earl Bauersack (right) appears with engineer Jack Dodrige (left) and unidentified passengers at a stop in front of La Jolla's Cabrillo Hotel. The gasoline train made frequent runs, stopping also in Pacific Beach and at Ramona's Marriage Place in Old Town, the latter considered a historic landmark for many visiting tourists.

PLUSH RIDE, 1909. The *Red Devil's* interior was an early-1900s statement in style and chic, as it provided a fashionable manner of travel. Round porthole windows could be opened for passengers to enjoy the countryside and the salty ocean breezes. The back of the car featured comfortable bench seating for a rear view as the train glided along the tracks.

Six

THE CIVIC COMMUNITY

On a warm August evening in 1915, an alarm signified that St. James-by-the-Sea Episcopal Church was on fire, and the dutiful fire department responded with its little engine and hoses. The fire was hardly quelled before another alarm went out that Eliza Virginia Scripps's cottage, the Iris, was aflame. Then all of Ellen Browning Scripps's estate on Prospect Street was smoking and flaming.

The year 1915 goes down in La Jolla history as the biggest fire year of all time. Homes, churches, and restaurants in the small village burned—mostly due to the work of an arsonist. But even in these early times, La Jolla's service and protection workers in the fire and police departments were ready for the call. The greatest challenge for police arrived in 1928, when a single bank robber wreaked havoc, firing a fusillade of shots up and down the streets before finally being shot himself by an officer.

With the start of World War I, another protective arm was at hand with thousands of soldiers stationed at nearby Camp Callan. La Jolla's early history is filled with the names of doctors, physicians, teachers, and scientists who contributed more than their share of services to the population of the few hundred citizens who came to call La Jolla their home.

CALL TO ALARM, C. 1910. Affectionately known as "Betsy," La Jolla's fire alarm bell of the early 1900s has an illustrious history. It was made in San Francisco especially for the San Diego Fire Department in 1885 and moved from San Diego to La Jolla in 1909. It rang for the first time to extinguish a blaze at the Cabrillo Hotel.

READY TO ROLL, C. 1910. Although La Jolla's first firefighters used horse-drawn equipment, a motor-operated vehicle was soon in coming. It was well equipped with hoses and ladders and had its own operating team: Lt. Frank Hayman (left) and firefighters Carl Sirl (center) and A. L. Salazar. Residential and commercial fires were a constant concern, especially when the hot Santa Ana winds infiltrated La Jolla's weather conditions.

LUCKY 13, 1913. The city constructed its first fire station, a one-story wood frame structure, on Herschel Avenue in 1913. Part of the San Diego Fire Department, La Jolla bore the designation of No. 13 in the line of succession around the area. Two years later, the station responded to the largest fire in La Jolla history, which destroyed Ellen Browning Scripps's estate and many other buildings.

MISSION-STYLE FIREHOUSE, 1930S. Architect Harry Abrams designed this Mission-style station, which was built by WPA workers in 1937. With two stories and a four-story tower, it stood on the same Herschel Avenue site as the previous station. The firehouse has since been restored for use as a community hall.

KEEPING ORDER, C. 1930. La Jolla police officers, part of the City of San Diego's overall force, operated out of the same headquarters as the fire department after the station was constructed on Herschel Avenue. Dinty Moore (center) was the officer in charge in 1928 when a sizable bank robbery rocked the town. The robber was shot dead as he tried to flee the town.

OFFICER IN CHARGE, 1917. Lucile Jeardeau, a La Jolla resident, was the first policewoman in the village, hired to monitor the visiting soldiers who were stationed nearby during World War I. She wore a brown jersey jacket and skirt when she walked her beat and had a badge clipped at the waist.

MAIL SERVICE, 1915. The first La Jolla postmaster, Charles H. Ritchie, was assigned to duty in 1894. In 1915, Nathan Rannells (left) assumed the post and remained for many years. This post office was located in a general store at 7824 Girard Avenue. Letters for delivery were addressed by cottage name until 1918, when house numbers were initiated.

SOLDIER BOYS, 1917. The U.S. Army set up a military base only a few miles north of La Jolla with the start of World War I. Known as Camp Kearny, it quickly grew to more than 24,000 soldiers, hundreds of whom came to La Jolla almost daily for respite from camp life. The soldiers enjoyed the beaches and sometimes conducted drills through the town.

LIFE IN CAMP, 1917. The Camp Kearny post consisted of makeshift tents set along dirt paths and roads on the high mesa beyond the La Jolla ocean cliffs. The dusty encampments were enhanced by a Hospitality House donated for the site by prominent La Jolla resident and philanthropist Ellen Browning Scripps.

MILITARY MIGHT, 1918. Camions with soldiers on the streets of La Jolla were a common sight during World War I, when the Camp Kearny encampment was only a few miles away. The Christmas parade of 1917 saw 25 trucks loaded with 50 men each from the camp, rolling down the street to the tune of "Tipperary."

ENJOYING THE SIGHTS, 1917. During World War I, it was remarked that La Jolla "was so homelike and appealing that it became renowned among the men" stationed at nearby Camp Kearny. Many of the servicemen came back to settle permanently in La Jolla after being impressed by the climate and location.

READY FOR THE ENEMY, 1918. As a protective measure for the village, World War I soldiers sometimes set up temporary encampments within the town. This one was located near the Children's Pool on Coast Boulevard in April 1918. When the war ended later that year, La Jolla staged a large celebration with the soldiers stationed here from all over the country.

MEDICAL AID, C. 1920. Dr. Samuel T. Gillespie established the first hospital in La Jolla (first known as the Sanitarium) in 1916. He practiced medicine in town for 18 years and was beloved in the community, participating in many organizations and civic affairs. Dr. Gillespie's hospital served as the nucleus for the Scripps Metabolic Clinic, which opened in 1924.

FIRST PHYSICIAN, C. 1910. Martha Dunn Corey moved to the La Jolla area in the 1890s and became the town's first physician. A graduate of the Woman's Homeopathic College of New York, she studied surgery in Birmingham, England, with the renowned surgeon Dr. Lawson Tait. In La Jolla, Corey established a general and obstetrical practice out of her home.

LEGAL COUNSEL, C. 1917. Jacob Chandler Harper, a leading figure in the Scripps newspaper chain for many years, moved to La Jolla after World War I in order to become Ellen Browning Scripps's legal counsel and personal agent. He figured prominently in the community and supervised many of the projects undertaken by Ellen Browning.

NATURALIST AND PHILOSOPHER, 1926. Dr. William Emerson Ritter founded the Scripps Institution of Oceanography in La Jolla and was an internationally known figure in marine science and zoology. He graduated from the University of California in 1888 and received his master's and doctorate degrees from Harvard University. Known for an uncanny eye when observing the world around him, Dr. Ritter entitled his last papers "The California Woodpecker and I."

READING, WRITING, AND ARITHMETIC, 1904. La Jolla had several very devoted teachers in its pioneer days, including Anna Harrison (left). She appears here with her class in front of the town's first schoolhouse, which was painted bright red and proverbially known as the Little Red Schoolhouse. It was located on Herschel Avenue.

EAGER (AND NOT SO EAGER) LEARNERS, 1906. Primary grades at the Little Red Schoolhouse are taught by Agnes Stitt (standing by blackboard) at the end of the school year in 1906. The Little Red Schoolhouse was the only educational facility in La Jolla until 1917, when the first building of the La Jolla Elementary School was completed.

Seven

ART AND PERFORMANCE

Largely due to the interest of early residents in education and culture, La Jolla grew up with an extraordinary history based in the cultural and literary arts. It was never quite the ordinary Western cow town identified by saloons and trading posts. Poets, musicians, artists, actors, and actresses flocked to La Jolla beginning in the 1890s with the establishment of the Green Dragon Colony by the German-born Anna Held.

Held was already known to the theatrical circuit abroad, having performed on the Shakespearean stage in London with well-known British actress Ellen Terry. Terry came to visit La Jolla, along with others in Held's retinue, and they were quick to share their theatrical and musical enthusiasm with the small community. The Green Dragon became the setting for classical music evenings, poetry readings, and other cultural programs.

Philanthropist Ellen Browning Scripps also added immensely to the community's cultural growth by commissioning architect Irving Gill to design buildings such as the La Jolla Woman's Club and the La Jolla Recreation Center to house theatrical productions in the early 20th century. The Woman's Club especially blossomed with costumed pageants and festivals, as well as serious theater such as the staging of the Greek tragedy *Agamemnon*, with Scripps in the title role. Through the 1920s, La Jolla was known for its plenitude of staged performances. Leading figures of the community were happy to put on costumes and enjoy an alternative theatrical life.

Movie culture arrived in La Jolla with the completion of the Granada Theater, an ornamental old palace with architectural trimmings of Morocco and Spain. The landmark theater on Girard was popular for young and old alike.

MUSICAL NOTES, 1898. The Green Dragon Colony was the nucleus of art and entertainment in La Jolla's early years, with proprietor Anna Held as the organizer. Held's Music Room, with its large piano, was often the gathering place for concerts and recitals, where the latest music was played along with the time-honored compositions of Bach and Beethoven.

TEA PARTY, C. 1900. Held's Green Dragon Colony was also a popular spot for children's tea parties. Village children enjoyed dainty cakes while Held hosted and brought dolls for the amusement of all. Her doll collection, known worldwide, served as the subject of "dress-up" photography in London studios.

SHAKESPEAREAN PAGEANT, 1916. The La Jolla Woman's Club frequently became the stage setting for costumed dramas starring leading figures from the small community. In April 1916, Dr. Mary B. Ritter (center) portrayed Queen Elizabeth at the spring season's Shakespearean Pageant. Weeks were spent assembling sets and costumes and rehearsing for "professional" performances.

GREEK TRAGEDY, 1916. For the fall season, village thespians chose a full-blown production of the Greek tragedy *Agamemnon*. The cast is assembled outside the La Jolla Woman's Club, where the play was staged on November 27, 1916. The all-female cast featured Ellen Browning Scripps (second row, second from left) in the title role of the tragic king who led the Greeks against Troy.

GREAT LEADER, 1916. Ellen Browning Scripps (left) was not only a great philanthropist to La Jolla but a true participant in the community. In 1916, she bravely undertook the lead role of Agamemnon in the production of the tragic Greek play.

VISITING THESPIAN, 1910. The well-known British actress Ellen Terry came to La Jolla in 1910 to visit the Green Dragon Colony and present a theater reading. She was also a guest at the Wheeler Bailey House, where she marveled over the Native American motifs and enjoyed an afternoon of Chopin and Grieg classical music. Terry was known in London especially for her Shakespearean roles.

SHAKESPEARE PRODUCTION, C. 1915. The La Jolla Woman's Club was the setting for numerous locally staged Shakespeare productions. Here the all-female cast for *Romeo and Juliet* poses beside the graceful arches of the clubhouse.

COLONIAL EVENING, 1916. Patriotism ran high in February 1916 when community leaders donned powdered wigs and finery to play prominent figures of the American Revolutionary period, including George and Martha Washington, Alexander Hamilton, John Adams, and Thomas Jefferson. The one-night performance was heralded as one of the most entertaining of the year in Southern California.

SWEET TIMES, 1918. The children of La Jolla gathered for Taffy Apple Day in 1918 in front of Chris's Market, where fruits, vegetables, and groceries were sold at "reasonable" prices. Taffy apples were the reason to dress in one's Sunday best, which ranged from frilly frocks and hats for the girls to breeches and white shirts for the boys.

OLD MAID'S PARTY, C. 1910. Not all the ladies participating were spinsters, but leading female figures of La Jolla found an occasion for frivolous celebration with an old maid's party. They included Olivia Mudgett (third from left), who as an early La Jolla realtor built one of the few Victorian-style houses in the village in the 1890s. Villa Waldo remains standing today on Drury Lane.

CHRISTMAS, 1900. Olivia Mudgett hosted a Christmas party for family and friends at her Villa Waldo home on December 25, 1900. The house was originally situated on Girard Avenue but was later moved to the back part of a lot on Drury Lane after Girard developed into a commercial street rather than a residential neighborhood.

PALESTINE PAGEANT, 1920.
Many different themes were
developed for the costumed
pageants popular in La Jolla from
1910 into the 1920s. Most of the
programs were staged at the newly
built La Jolla Woman's Club or at
the La Jolla Recreation Center,
also newly built at the time and
designed by architect Irving Gill.
H. Martin wore an imposing
costume as a Bedouin in one
such pageant.

ESTHER PAGEANT, 1924. The
pageant of *Esther the Beautiful
Queen* was staged and directed by
Countess Laura de Turczynowicz
at the La Jolla Woman's Club
in 1924. The countess (center,
next to pony) also organized the
La Jolla Opera Company in the
1920s and directed a number
of operettas under its aegis,
including *The Pirates of Penzance*
and *Hansel and Gretel*.

QUEEN ELIZABETH, 1916. In April of this year, La Jolla women gathered to present an elaborate Shakespeare festival that featured practically every female citizen impersonating prominent characters from the bard's many plays. The festival was staged at the La Jolla Woman's Club. Dr. Mary Ritter played a major role as Queen Elizabeth. Later that spring, the group planted a northern oak Shakespeare tree on the grounds.

LINCOLN CENTENNIAL, 1909. Scripps Park at La Jolla Cove was the setting for a flag-raising ceremony on February 12, 1909, celebrating the centennial of Pres. Abraham Lincoln's birth. It featured the reading of Lincoln's Gettysburg Address and the singing of "The Star Spangled Banner" and "The Battle Hymn of the Republic." A Confederate veteran was called upon to unfurl the flag, but his age forced deferment of the duty to another program participant.

FLAG RAISING, 1918. Ellen Browning Scripps (seated in wicker chair) attended a flag raising in 1918 that called attention to the influenza epidemic. Face masks were worn from October 25 to November 17 and December 6 to 25 that year to combat the spread of influenza. The masks did not encumber the celebration of Thanksgiving and Christmas, as the dates conveniently allowed them to be removed.

LAST SPIKE, 1894. The driving of the last spike, marking the arrival of the railroad and train service from downtown San Diego, was cause for a large celebration on May 15, 1894. Emma Harris drove the spike at the boisterous 1890s scene, which took place on Prospect Street near Draper Avenue, with music bands and various outdoor sports competitions like high jump and hurdles.

FIFTY YEARS LATER, 1944. La Jollans celebrated the 50th anniversary of the driving of the last spike with a presentation on the La Jolla Woman's Club stage. W. C. Crandall (center, with black coat and bowler hat) officiated. Ironically, the railroad had lost its importance to La Jolla as a means of bringing people to town, as the automobile had become the major transport.

FLICKS MATINEE, 1934. The Granada Theater was the epitome of the grand old movie houses in La Jolla, with an ornate interior resplendent after a Spanish-Moorish theme. It played to full houses and was a popular venue for children's matinees such as this one on Christmas Day. The movie theater was a prominent architectural feature on Girard for many years.

POET LAUREATE, C. 1930S. After they moved to the village from Emporia, Kansas, writer and poet Walt Mason and his wife, Ella, frequently entertained and held workshops at their La Jolla home through the 1930s. Walt contributed regularly to La Jolla newspapers and was a familiar local character on the streets, where he could be spotted walking daily with a beloved cocker spaniel named Red.

LIVE PERFORMANCE, 1926. The Granada Theater stage served as the setting for a live performance of *The Dictator*, presented by the American Legion in the spring of 1926. It featured an all-male cast of prominent businessmen and community leaders, including Alfred Iller, Dr. A. B. Smith, Fred Howard, Ben Genter, and Elden McFarland.

Eight

THE SPORTING SCENE

Two entirely divergent sports activities occupied pioneer La Jollans in the late 19th and early 20th centuries: golf and competitive ocean swimming. History has failed to record exactly what encouraged the small La Jolla population to try to lay out a putting green along the barren coast; nevertheless, in the 1890s, they took shovels and the necessary measuring devices in hand to create a small course at Prospect Street where it intercepts with Silverado Street and Exchange Place. Anson Mills recorded having a delightful time playing on the course in his diaries, despite the absence of grass. Ladies and gentlemen were photographed with their clubs and golf balls, the latter of which they made by hand of compressed rubber.

Competitive swimming took off in 1916 with the start of the annual La Jolla Rough Water Swim—a tradition that continues nearly 100 years later. It was originally called the Biological Pier Swim because the course began at the Biological Pier in La Jolla Shores (now Scripps Institution of Oceanography) and ended at La Jolla Cove. Many top swimmers and personalities competed in the event through the years, including Florence Chambers, Buster Crabbe, and Max Miller.

The opening of La Jolla High School in 1922 brought a great variety of other sports for the enjoyment of both spectators and participants. They included tennis, baseball, basketball, and football. The new La Jolla Recreation Center, opened in 1915 after a generous donation by philanthropist Ellen Browning Scripps, also encouraged many community sports, especially tennis. Meanwhile, the campus of the privately owned Bishop's School for Girls was the setting for sports befitting a young women's institution. Riding classes and gymnastics were the proper athletic pursuits.

ROUGH WATER SWIM, c. 1940. The most well-established, consistently presented sports event in La Jolla is the Rough Water Swim, first held in 1916 and continuing to the present day. Top swimmers numbering in the hundreds compete in the mile-and-three-quarter course, which runs from the cove to near Scripps Pier. New records are set each year.

SURFING, c. 1940. La Jolla's Windansea Beach began to be known as a prime surfing spot in the 1930s, when locals built their own boards to ride the challenging and unpredictable waves. The beach became immortalized in the 1960s with the publication of Tom Wolfe's *The Pump House Gang*, heralding the cultural revolution of the time.

SURF SHACK. Built of palm fronds and salvaged timbers, the Wind 'n' Sea Surf Shack, at the foot of Neptune Street, became a landmark for the sport of surfing through the years. High tides washed it away, but a dedicated surfing group always gathered to rebuild and once decided to laud the shack with historic designation as an important icon of the community.

SYNCHRONIZED SWIMMING, c. 1940. Bathing beauties form a circle for a synchronized swimming session at the La Jolla Beach and Tennis Club. The club in La Jolla Shores was a popular gathering spot for many different sports through the decades. It began as the La Jolla Beach and Yacht Club, though tennis soon took precedence.

MR. TENNIS, 1916. Although he started work in La Jolla with a law office, Archie Carlisle Talboy became director of the La Jolla Recreation Center shortly after it was built and remained in the position for many years. Among his many achievements was the organization of a tennis tournament that eventually led to him being known as "Mr. Tennis." He also headed many other sports.

MAKING WAVES, C. 1915. The original La Jolla Playground (later renamed Recreation Center) featured a children's wading pool covered by a pergola and an adjacent sandbox for play. The pool was eliminated when benefactor Ellen Browning Scripps created the Children's Pool, which was protected by a seawall at a nearby beach.

TEAM PLAYERS, 1923. Assembled just a year after La Jolla High School opened, these young athletes comprised the first Viking team to participate in interscholastic competition. They put together their own uniforms and were the pride of Principal Buel F. Enyeart (far right). The first senior graduating class in 1926 had 11 students.

FOOTBALL TEAM, 1927–1928. La Jolla High School's football team practiced on a dirt field under the supervision of coach Clarence Johnson, who was in charge of all men's athletics. The field constituted five acres, half of which was purchased outright by the San Diego City School Board. The other half was donated to the school by Ellen Browning Scripps, La Jolla resident and well-known philanthropist.

TENNIS TEAM, 1926. La Jolla High School's first tennis team was coeducational in 1926, the same year that the initial class was graduated. Besides the coed tennis team, the girls' athletic program featured volleyball and baseball teams. The men's consisted of baseball, track, swimming, football, basketball, and track.

BOYS' SWIMMING, 1929. Though La Jolla High School was without a swimming pool in its early years, the fact hardly kept the school from having a swim team since the Pacific Ocean was only a few blocks away. The team frequently worked out in the waves and built up extraordinary strength. By 1934, it had won five straight conference championships.

BASKETBALL, 1928. In the 1920s, La Jolla High School's basketball team was divided into four divisions, including this C team, which came close to winning county championship laurels in 1928. When the final counts were in, however, La Jolla was beaten by Roosevelt Junior High School 16-14 after the game went into two extra periods.

TENNIS, 1929. With the opening of the La Jolla Beach and Tennis Club in the 1920s and with the ample courts available at the La Jolla Recreation Center, tennis grew as a popular sport for both young and old. La Jolla High School's tennis team, seen finely fitted in this photograph, included both male and female athletes.

GYMNASTICS, 1922. In the foreground of architect Irving Gill's modern design for the campus buildings, Bishop's School girls practice formal gymnastics on an outdoor lawn. Run by a headmistress, the school had a reputation as one of the finest educational facilities in the country. It remains privately run and has been coeducational now for many years.

RIDING CLASS, 1928. The Bishop's School began as a private school for young women, who participated in athletics suitable to a social set. Riding classes were among the activities encouraged, and the Bishop's girls were a common sight around La Jolla, trotting their horses through dirt streets and vacant lots dressed in formal riding gear.

BASKETBALL, 1929. The basketball court was located outside on a dirt field at La Jolla High School in the 1920s. The rough-and-tumble games were played with great spirit in competition with other educational institutions throughout San Diego County. The school was known for excellence in many sports, but especially basketball.

GIRLS' BASEBALL, 1926. It might have been known as a boys' game, but baseball was an important girls' sport at La Jolla High School in the 1920s as well. Girls also had organized teams for volleyball, swimming, and tennis. The girls brought home a San Diego County volleyball championship in 1926 for the second consecutive year.

COVE SWIMMING, 1917. The sometimes rough waters at La Jolla Cove provided a likely location for swimmers to practice their strokes, even if the required bathing suits were somewhat restricting. La Jolla passed a bathing suit ordinance in 1917 that defined propriety not only on the beaches, but also on the streets.

LADY FISHERMAN, 1903. Virtually as soon as La Jolla's early visitors and residents arrived, they found the sea an ample resource for food and recreation. La Jolla Shores (then called Long Beach) was a favorite area for throwing a line into the ocean and hopefully being rewarded with a tasty marine specimen for dinner. In diaries recalling life in La Jolla, Anson Mills often wrote about spending his days fishing and coming home with exceptional catches.

SHOOTING SCENE, C. 1900. The wild, rugged cliffs around Torrey Pines State Park provided a destination for small hunting parties in the early 1900s. Rabbits and rattlesnakes were easy game if one chose to hunt or shoot for sport. Hunting parties also left from the La Jolla area on greater excursions into San Diego's east county, where larger game and fowl could be found.

PRACTICE SHOT, C. 1910. Kitty Murray, a nearby resident at Cave and Prospect, practices a golf shot on La Jolla's first course at Prospect where it intersects with Exchange and Silverado. She sponsored the launching of the *Viking* fishing boat in 1906 after it was built by two Scandinavian fishermen.

HOLE IN ONE, 1890s. Golf became a popular sport in La Jolla as early as the 1890s, when a putting green of sorts was created on the dirt streets at Prospect where it intersects with Exchange and Silverado. In 1901, a golf club was formed in La Jolla. Golfers used only about four clubs and frequently made their own balls by boiling rubber and pressing it into a mold.

DIVING, 1898. It was for both sport and spectacle that Horace Poole made several dives into the ocean from high above the cliffs at Goldfish Point. The dives were done on the Fourth of July in the 1890s and early 1900s to attract people to La Jolla and promote it as a place to live. On one occasion, Poole drenched himself with kerosene and dived as a flaming fireball. He died a peaceable death in 1943.

Nine

HOUSES AND
ARCHITECTURE

Although Victorian and Queen Anne architecture permeated much residential design throughout California in the 1890s, little of it was evidenced in La Jolla, where the seaside location encouraged a simpler style of building commonly known as the California bungalow. Houses were single-story, single-wall constructions with interiors commonly of unfinished board-and-batten redwood. Wood shingles sometimes covered the exterior facade. Hip roofs and veranda-style or open-front porches were other common features. Such bungalows dotted the La Jolla coastline through the late 19th and early 20th centuries. This style is seen in the houses forming the Green Dragon Colony and remnants of other early bungalows such as the Brockton Villa and the Red Roost and Red Rest at La Jolla Cove.

The simple vernacular architecture changed gradually as Spanish Colonial Revival and Mission designs became popular, inspired in part by San Diego's Panama-California Exposition of 1915–1916 in Balboa Park. Modernism also gained a foothold and was reflected in residences designed by architects Irving Gill (Ellen Browning Scripps's second home) and Rudolph Schindler (El Pueblo Rivera).

As La Jolla grew into the 1920s and 1930s with the arrival of wealth, a host of new architects began to set an eclectic pattern for residential design. These included William Templeton Johnson, Edgar Ullrich, Thomas Shepherd, Lillian Rice, and Herbert and Florence Palmer. The rich variety of their architectural styles was seen in the major subdivisions of the era like the Barber Tract, the Muirlands, and La Jolla Shores. Houses they designed ranged from Mediterranean villas to English Tudor cottages to Spanish Colonial estates to homes rooted in the tradition of the American Cape Cod. Set in the lush landscape of palm trees and exotic flora, their designs formed the backbone of the multi-patterned neighborhoods that make up present-day La Jolla: great mansions mixed with tidy cottages adjacent to sandy and rocky beaches.

BROCKTON VILLA, 1894. Originally built as a seaside retreat by San Diego physician Dr. Joseph Rodes, Brockton Villa dates to 1894. After Rodes's 1896 death, the house became a beach rental for many years, known for its superb location above La Jolla Cove. With a veranda-style porch and hip roof, it is considered a prime example of bungalow architecture. It has found new use today as a restaurant.

RED REST, 1895. Another good example of bungalow architecture, Red Rest was constructed across from the cove and adjacent to another cottage, known as Red Roost. It is one of only a handful built in early La Jolla that remain today. The cottage is representative of the first indigenous domestic architecture in California, predating vernacular prototypes designed by architects such as Greene and Greene in Pasadena.

WISTERIA COTTAGE, 1904. Named for the wisteria-covered entry pergola that cascades with purple blossoms each spring, this house was acquired by Eliza Virginia Scripps shortly after completion and remains in the Scripps family. Reminiscent of early bungalow or Craftsman architecture, it was redesigned by architect Irving Gill in 1909, at which point loggias were added and the front porch enclosed.

BARBER HOUSE, 1922. Philip Barber, an investor from New Jersey, purchased extensive property along the sand dunes south of the village in 1921 and hired architect Herbert Palmer to design an expansive Mediterranean-style home. Finished in 1922, it became the Barber family home for many years. Barber developed other property in the area known today as La Jolla's Barber Tract.

VILLA WALDO, 1894. One of the few two-story houses built in early La Jolla, this home originally served as a private residence for realtor Olivia Mudgett. It was frequently a gathering place for social activities when La Jolla had only a few residents and consisted of dirt roads with no streets or sidewalks. Mudgett was the widow of a Maine sea captain and the sister of another pioneer La Jolla woman, Nellie Mills.

THE TAJ, 1927. In the 1920s, architect Herbert Palmer designed several significant residences in La Jolla, but the most unusual was this landmark building on Torrey Pines Road, which he created as his home. He named it Casa de Las Joyas (House of Jewels), but La Jollans fondly called it the Taj Mahal for its resemblance to an *Arabian Nights* palace. Palmer was the natural son of Great Britain's Prince of Wales, Queen Victoria's heir who later became Edward VII.

TAJ DETAIL, 1927. Palmer considered his home a personal temple and designed a peaceful entrance composed of columns and arches reminiscent of India and Morocco. The surfaces are inscribed with philosophic meditations related to Indian mysticism. One of the main features of the house is a meditation dome consisting of a circular room with windows framing tranquil views of the Pacific Ocean.

MUIR HOUSE, 1927. Architect Edgar Ullrich designed a magnificent Spanish-style residence surrounded by orchards and flora for H. J. Muir, who had purchased 257 acres for development in the hills above La Jolla in the 1920s. The lots offered expansive ocean views, as did Muir's own home. The stock market crash of 1929 and the subsequent Depression forestalled Muir's plans, however, and he was forced to sell his property.

SOUSA HOUSE, C. 1920. The family of "March King" John Philip Sousa lived in this home for many years. It was built on Draper Avenue and designed by architect Irving Gill using the same tilt-up concrete construction Gill had introduced in other structures in the area, such as the La Jolla Woman's Club and the Recreation Center.

WINDEMERE, C. 1900. Gill's early house designs in La Jolla included this cottage, built for an Englishman named John Kendall. Windemere first stood on Prospect Street but was later moved to Virginia Way. Writer Beatrice Harraden, who lived in it for some time, is believed to have composed two novels here: *Marrying Moods* and *Ships That Pass in the Night.*

CALIFORNIA-MEDITERRANEAN, C. 1930S. Architect Thomas Shepherd traveled extensively in the Mediterranean and came to La Jolla to practice his trade in 1926. He designed about 200 residences, many inspired by his travels but with typical red-tiled roofs and patios to accommodate Southern California living. He considered La Jolla "a community of conservative and classic quality" and designed many homes to reflect this sentiment.

AMBIENT DETAILS, C. 1930. Reflecting the architectural concept that "God is in the details," La Jolla architect Thomas Shepherd designed many residences with intimate entries and door and window effects. This home features several leaded-glass windows and a trademark Shepherd interior including a salon-style living room that is far grander in scope than the other rooms.

TUDOR TOUCH, C. 1930. Although many of Shepherd's residential designs were inspired by the Mediterranean, he also exercised a great deal of architectural dexterity. This cottage was built in the Barber Tract and illustrates the Tudor Revival style popular in a particular neighborhood through the 1920s and 1930s. The small walled rose garden at the front entry evokes the mood of a typical English cottage.

GARDEN SETTING, 1904. Despite the scarcity of water in early La Jolla, the sunny, warm climate encouraged home builders to surround themselves with interesting botanical life ranging from ficus hedges to exotic specimens. This two-story bungalow, constructed of board-and-batten redwood, was named Sunnycrest in keeping with the surrounding cheery garden at Ivanhoe Avenue and Prospect Street.

ALL GROWN UP, C. 1920S. Built at 1448 Torrey Pines Road, this house is another example of how profusely gardens grew in the pioneer seaside community when they were tended and planted. Ficus fairly obscures the front of the house, along with a tree and shrubs planted at the entry. The building served for many years as the home of the Union Congregational Church rector.

SPARSE LANDSCAPE, C. 1900. This photograph, showing the dirt roadways leading into La Jolla, illustrates how few houses were built along the cliffs when La Jolla was first subdivided. The houses were scattered, few and far between, with only the newly planted telephone poles connecting them. La Jolla Cove appears to the far right middle of the view.

GRAY RESIDENCE, 1928. In the late 1920s, Gordon Gray built this elaborate home in the La Jolla Shores area after a design by architect Thomas Shepherd. For many years, Gray served as president of the Art Center, established in 1941, which would become the nucleus of the San Diego Museum of Contemporary Art on Prospect Street. The property included a door entering the side of a cliff protrusion and leading to a seawater aquarium.

DEVANNEY HOUSE, C. 1900. Sam Devanney arrived in La Jolla in 1902 and built one of the first permanent homes on Park Row. His mother was an originator of the Old Ladies of La Jolla Club. The Devanneys also owned one of the first automobiles in La Jolla and had a single-car detached garage specially built on their property. Park Row was part of the original La Jolla Park subdivision created by Francis Terrell Botsford in 1887.

WOOSTER HOUSE, C. 1920. Located at 1375 Park Row, this residence was one of the many early homes in La Jolla built by Charlie Stratton, a well-known local builder. The photograph shows the kind of hands-on building typical of the period and the simple framing of a large two-story structure with a hip roof. The house was built for Dorothy Wooster, who later married Berton William Sibley, a highly decorated World War I hero.

WALT MASON HOUSE, 1920. A popular writer and poet, Walt Mason moved to La Jolla from Emporia, Kansas, in 1920 and built this snug bungalow for himself and his family at 1411 Virginia Way. He was one of La Jolla's best-known and beloved citizens, residing here until his death in 1939. He wrote a regular column for the local newspaper called "Rippling Rhymes."

EDGE HILL, C. 1910. Paul Chase, the son of one of La Jolla's first merchants, built this home at 1533 Virginia Way in 1907–1908. It has some of the finest Craftsman detailing of this particular period, featuring a wide-overhang, low gable roof with open rafter tails. A wide pair of dormers peeks out from under the shed roofs. The entrance pergola of heavy cut timbers is supported by rock columns with concrete caps. The same rock serves as a railing on either side of the front entrance stairs.

EASTMAN HOUSE, 1924. Situated at 7620 Draper Avenue, this house typifies the California bungalows that lined the streets around the immediate area of the village through the first part of the 20th century. It was purchased in 1924 by Dr. William Easton, who practiced medicine in La Jolla for more than 20 years and owned this house for more than 40.

TURRET HOUSE, 1904. Somewhat of an anomaly, this small Victorian-style house with turret is believed to have stood for a short time at the corner of Silverado Street and Draper Avenue. Only a handful of Victorians were ever built in La Jolla, as the bungalow was frequently considered more amenable to seaside living. What happened to this residence remains a mystery.

HEALD HOUSE, 1887. Believed to be the first house actually constructed in La Jolla, this home, located at Silverado and Exchange, took advantage of ocean views toward Goldfish Point and La Jolla Cove. It was built by early resident George Webster Heald during 1887, the same year that La Jolla's first lots were auctioned and the town was founded.

ACROSS AMERICA, PEOPLE ARE DISCOVERING
SOMETHING WONDERFUL. THEIR HERITAGE.

Arcadia Publishing is the leading local history publisher in the United States. With more than 4,000 titles in print and hundreds of new titles released every year, Arcadia has extensive specialized experience chronicling the history of communities and celebrating America's hidden stories, bringing to life the people, places, and events from the past. To discover the history of other communities across the nation, please visit:

www.arcadiapublishing.com

Customized search tools allow you to find regional history books about the town where you grew up, the cities where your friends and family live, the town where your parents met, or even that retirement spot you've been dreaming about.

MAP SEARCH

* 9 7 8 1 5 3 1 6 3 7 2 3 1 *